[illegible] Text Guide

by

Ross Huggard

(M Ed Pol Admin, B Ec, Dip Ed, Grad Dip Ed Admin)

Fred D'Aguiar's

The Longest Memory

This edition first published in 1998 by
Insight Publications Pty Ltd
ACN 005 102 983
PO Box 130
Drouin Victoria 3818
Australia.
☎ 03 5625 1701

Editing by Iris Breuer

Design and DTP by Geoffrey Heard & Associates ✆ (03) 9583 0788

Printed by Australian Print Group, Maryborough, Victoria.

Huggard, Ross

Insight text guide: Fred D'Aguiar's The Longest Memory.

Bibliography

ISBN 1 875882 10 3

D'Aguiar, Fred, 1960- . Longest memory. 2. D'Aguiar, Fred. 1960- . – Criticism and Interpretation. I. Title. II Title: Longest memory.

823.914

The editors and publishers wish to acknowledge the kind permission of Vintage (Random House Australia) to reprint material from *The Longest Memory* by Fred D'Aguiar.

CONTENTS

INTRODUCTION

Frank D'Aguiar's novel, *The Longest Memory*[1], recounts the story of the slave Whitechapel whose remarkable and long life straddles the 18th and 19th centuries. His white master, Mr Whitechapel, and his black fellow slaves perceive him to be the elder statesman of the slaves — a man of wisdom and insight.

While Whitechapel, the slave, is at the centre of this novel, the book is written from a number of viewpoints. It offers a series of accounts of life on the Whitechapel plantation in Virginia in the late 1700s and early 1800s with its focus on the circumstances of the whipping to death of Chapel, a young runaway slave.

The plot is not unfolded in strict chronological sequence, reminding us of the way in which the past (and our recollection of it in our memories) so often determines and influences the present and future in the complex tapestry of our lives. Through both Whitechapel and the plantation owners, it becomes clear that the living link between the past and their present is the old slave himself, who has been symbolically and shrewdly named after the current plantation owner's father. He has observed first hand the way in which the social and economic system of slavery has evolved through almost a century. He is like a living time capsule, an agent of memory. If, as Mr Whitechapel asserts to his non-conformist daughter, Lydia, it may be 'the next century' (p. 88) before she and her beloved Chapel can 'sit and read together', many more memories will need to be created before slavery truly can end.

Yet, by the end of the novel, it is clear to us that slavery is not destined to last much longer; a fact even recognised by the controlling whites as represented by the plantation owners and the editor of their paper, *The Virginian*. Chapel's gruesome death will not stem the flow of agitation or the talk of Abolitionists (those who advocated that slavery be abolished and outlawed). Old Whitechapel's own pathetic death seems to signal the end of an era and register change to the prevailing social order.

---

1 D'Aguiar, *The Longest Memory*, Vintage, Random House Australia, Sydney, 1995. All references are to this edition.

CONTEXT & BACKGROUND

The Rise of Slavery in North America

Without an understanding of the reasons for the advent of black slavery in North America, one cannot really appreciate the canvas that lies so conspicuously behind this text.

It was the enforced slavery of African blacks, captured by slave-traders off the coast of West Africa from the 1600s onwards, which was not only to change the course of American history, but also to fuel the Civil War of the 1860s. Slavery was also one of the most obvious and palpable signs of different values between the Northern and Southern states, since it was the agricultural South which so depended upon and so strongly advocated the use of slavery over its 250 or so years of existence.

Given the enormous distance between America and its crucial European markets, the North American settlers soon reasoned that they must somehow cut the costs of their production to make exporting profitable. They concluded that if they were to reduce their labour costs substantially, then they could really make an impact upon the European markets. The farming practised in the Southern states, the key rural states, was centred on the cultivation of valuable cash crops — cotton especially, and sugar and tobacco — which all required very large workforces for cultivating and harvesting and so led to the demand for cheap labour which the prolific African slave supply satisfied.

Why use labour from a far-off continent?

Firstly, these Africans were in such abundant supply that they could apparently satisfy the huge needs for labour on the Southern plantations. Secondly, they were seen to be hard working and cheap to acquire, coupled with the fact that many of them possessed valuable farming skills. Thirdly, unlike the Native Americans, they were apparently largely resistant to endemic European diseases. Fourthly, these West African people were not protected by any recognised legal system and thus could effectively be forcibly apprehended to work as desired by any North American colonists. So, between 1619 and 1664, slavery became institutionalised, firstly in the Southern State of Maryland. It is important to appreciate these reasons when considering the attitude of the other white plantation owners to Mr Whitechapel, and the extent to which they perceived him to be a threat to the established order in their society.

The Legal and Moral Domination of Slaves

Under new laws in the Deep South, the employer purchased not simply the labour of their servants, but their bodies. Their children could also be sold and bought as the white owners wished. Known as chattel slaves, they owned nothing. This formalisation of the concept of chattel slaves established most powerfully the possibility of the total exploitation of black African slaves.

The laws of many Southern states also nominated harsh punishments for 'crimes' such as the stealing of food (a minimum of 40 lashes for the first offence) and attempted escape. If a slave resisted capture and was subsequently killed, the owner could claim compensation from the state government as the slave had no rights in such circumstances. As early as 1669 in Virginia the law went further: a white killing a slave was a non-criminal act and hence went unpunished.

The final element to ensure the total domination of black African slaves in North America came with the moral justifications that developed to excuse the appalling treatment many whites inflicted on their slaves. For example, it was stated that these blacks were inferior to their white masters, and, in some sense 'sub-human' and 'uncivilised', with their distinctive dark skin cited as concrete evidence of their inferior and different racial state. This was, of course, a remarkable sign of self-interest triumphing over moral principles. The colonial churches of the time essentially supported the rise of slavery, arguing that slaves could be converted to be true Christians and yet remain slaves, given that they were inferior beings in God's eyes. They were instructed to be willingly compliant to the wishes of their superior white masters, since God would prepare a mansion in heaven for them. Many ministers of religion assured their white congregations that God approved of slavery to 'improve' such inferior blacks, whilst blacks were told that acceptance of their slave status was a pre-requisite for eternal salvation.

Attitudes of Main Characters to Slavery

Characters' attitudes to slavery present opposing positions. The plantation owners, Sanders Senior and Junior support slavery unconditionally, Mr Whitechapel is more lenient but still clearly favours

it; the old slave Whitechapel counsels obedience to white masters while Chapel and Lydia oppose slavery.

In the context of the period, Whitechapel's apparently willing acceptance of his 90 years as a slave is more readily understandable — he sees obedience as the best principle to gain co-operation from white overseers. Lydia and Chapel, through their love for each other and through Chapel's literacy, openly resist. Their relationship challenges the very foundations of whites' justification for the establishment and continuation of slavery.

Mr Whitechapel perceives the treatment of his plantation's blacks to be essentially moral and Christian although in the light of other plantation owners' attitudes, he is certainly more humane, believing that 'a satisfied slave is a happy slave and a more productive worker' (p. 29). However, in the system as it developed, fear of unrest was used to justify whippings and more brutal practices incompatible with Christian beliefs, issues that are discussed in chapter 11, *The Virginian*.

Extent of Slavery

By 1790, well over one-fifth of the United States' population was made up of black slaves. These slaves were overwhelmingly concentrated in the plantation-dominated Southern States, with 86% being held in Virginia, North and South Carolina and Maryland.

In Virginia, the location of Mr Whitechapel's plantation, slavery rapidly spread — from only 12,000 in 1708 to 259,000 in 1782. In South Carolina, from the early 1700s until well after the Civil War of the 1860s, the black population actually exceeded that of the white population.

The Northern States, with significantly fewer slaves, abolished slavery in the years 1787-1804. As a consequence, slavery became an issue between the Northern industrialists and the Southern plantation owners, eventually becoming a major source of conflict that led to the Civil War. Freedom for slaves in the North is important in the novel. It fuels Lydia and Chapel's hopes of making a life together in the North if Chapel can escape.

Resistance and Rebellion among Slaves

Larger numbers of slaves, worsening relations between plantation owners, their overseers and their slaves and the harsher penalties for minor and major 'crimes' led to growing unrest among slaves in the South.

The economic demand for cotton production cemented slavery into the Southern way of life. Plantations grew ever larger in the late 1700s and early 1800s, and as a result, ever-larger numbers of slaves were needed. The once personal relationships between slave and master were typically eroded, evident as more and more slave overseers were required to manage them. This often significantly worsened race relations. At the same time, acts of non-compliance by slaves, including sabotage, go-slows and theft from their master (which was to them only reclaiming what was rightfully theirs) increased in their frequency. The other common form of effective rebellion was, of course, to run away. As is only too apparent in the case of Chapel's hapless attempt at escape in the novel, the chance of success was always very limited without being able to access an organised network (the so-called 'Underground Railroad' did emerge as a reasonably successful route at a later stage).

The ultimate form of slave resistance remained that of outright revolt. Black Americans planned three major revolts. The most relevant here is the first in Richmond, Virginia, in 1800. It involved 1,000 slaves, but never actually materialised. This was partly because cities such as Richmond had substantial black populations often outnumbering their white counterparts who often lived in more flexible and bearable domestic situations than rural slaves. Such urban black slaves nevertheless worked equally hard for their white masters.

Slavery, Literacy and Freedom

Literacy gives individuals power — something slave owners realised fully when they prevented slaves from learning to read and write.

A time-honoured mechanism for controlling others deemed less worthy or important is to keep them ill educated and, most of all, illiterate. We may not perceive the ability to read and write to be special and yet for millions in developing countries even today, a lack of literacy continues to be an enormous barrier to progress and independence. So it was for the black slaves in the Deep South since it was presumed that they were inferior beings. Acquiring any form of literacy was a distinct possibility only for some of the domestic slaves who had to shop for their masters.

In the novel we can see that Chapel's quite consummate literacy skills present him with an important potential asset for freedom, a reality not lost upon either his proud mother who says, 'My son can open a book and sound like the master' (p. 85) or upon his outraged master, who beats Chapel and warns Lydia. Mr Whitechapel's attitude is encapsulated in his words to the editor of *The Virginian*: 'The father said it filled a slave with discontent when he can read about the world but must live on a plantation as a slave and see nothing of that world' (p. 117). This logic is rather reminiscent of that of lords in medieval Europe who so consciously sought to keep their agrarian serfs illiterate in order to keep them compliant and relatively content with their very hard lifestyle.

The Abolition of Slavery

In the early 1800s, an ever-growing abolition movement began in the Northern States. It steadily gained momentum, as the North became a logical target and haven for black slaves who successfully escaped from the South.

The outlawing of slavery in the Northern States (between 1787 and 1804) brought them into direct potential conflict with their Southern counterparts. Indeed, it can be said that a fundamental cause of the American Civil War (1861–1865) was the issue of slavery, although at the time the Confederate Southern States claimed that they were fundamentally concerned about their rights as states in the Union. In reality they were more concerned about whether they would be able to retain slavery as members of the Union.

This novel, set in America at the outset of the 19th century, then sits at the crossroads in the practice of black slavery. After over 150 years of this abhorrent practice, there can be little doubt that many Southerners were all too aware that the calls for abolishing slavery were getting louder in the increasingly prosperous and now unified North. Moreover, greater disquiet amongst slaves was becoming more prevalent. This resulted in some cases of increasingly brutal forms of white retaliation as a warning, as we see in the tragic case of Chapel. The forces on both sides of the moral and economic divide were gathering for an historic showdown. All of this forms the backdrop to the novel.

Given that this supposedly civilised and Christian society could have been so centred upon slavery remains the prominent and most disturbingly irrational image; it must surely be seen to lie at the heart of this remarkably resonant novel. Clearly the issue of slavery and the treatment of blacks is still pre-eminent in the consciousness of many Americans, as reflected in the words of President Bill Clinton at his re-election in January 1997: "The divide of race has been America's constant curse."

Genre

***The Longest Memory** is a novel that uses a method of multiple narration whereby characters speak from their own viewpoint in a particular language either directly or through diary extracts. Newspaper articles are also used to present other voices and views.*

The novel is like a tapestry, the threads weaving in different perspectives of the main events and people in Whitechapel's life. This creates a powerful sense of history, not history that represents the past as 'linear progression', but rather history that is full of contradictions, a series of upheavals that can leap backwards and forwards. In *The Longest Memory*, the resources of the historian — personal and official — are combined with the imaginative resources of the fiction writer.

Fred D'Aguiar comments on how history not only finds evidence of things past but also enables us to see gaps in the records — absences.[2] We realise that such silences have arisen because people's suffering has been so acute that memory has been repressed in order for them to survive. For old Whitechapel, remembering a past means re-living that past in which the pain of human cruelty and his own mistakes are embedded.

While novelists draw on history in various ways, they also use imagination to re-create a particular past. D'Aguiar in this novel fills some of the silences surrounding both the African slaves and their white masters through re-imagining that past. Hence, *The Longest Memory* projects us imaginatively into the minds of an illiterate slave, Whitechapel, and his young illiterate wife, Cook, a plantation owner, Mr Whitechapel, his overseers, Sanders Senior and Junior, his daughter, Lydia, and a literate mixed-race slave, Chapel, who rebels against the slavery of his people but dies in the effort. It reveals the unjust treatment of slaves, the rape of Cook, the beating to death of Chapel, the illicit love affair between Lydia, the white master's daughter, and Chapel, the literate slave, and the attitudes of the people who perpetuate slavery. Further, it explores the mental states of slavery for both whites and blacks.

---

2 Mary-Ann Metcalf, *Fred D'Aguiar, Author Interview*, Random House, Australia, 1996 p. 1

Structure

The form of the novel reflects D'Aguiar's concept of history as he abandons the single viewpoint of a linear structure for multiple perspectives. Nine chapters proper present stories told by the characters themselves, each in the first person, and chapter 3 uses the diary form to reveal Sanders Senior's private thoughts on important elements of his own life. A series of editorials in chapter 11, *The Virginian*, reveal Southern whites' attitudes of the time towards central issues of slavery. These eleven chapters are enveloped in the reflections of old Whitechapel — 'Remembering' and 'Forgetting'.

Comments on the Structure

The multiple narratives, or chain of voices, each add to our understanding of the history, not only of the Whitechapel Plantation, but also of Virginia of the time. In using this structure, D'Aguiar has also carefully interlocked and sequenced the narratives presented. The central motif of memory is dramatised through old Whitechapel's voice in 'Remembering' and 'Forgetting' at the beginning and the end of the novel which act as virtual 'bookends' to the narrative.

It is most significant, of course, that the opening and closing words and ideas in the text come directly from old Whitechapel. He is the pivotal character around whom all else seems to revolve directly or indirectly. Structurally, it is crucial that he opens the novel by remembering the horror he has brought upon himself. It now haunts him as he longs to escape his painful memories and to die. At the end of the text, he is finally forgetting, reconciling himself to his pain; he can die in relative peace.

The sequencing of the thirteen numbered chapters is also of note. The central character, Whitechapel, presents the hideous conundrum of his situation; after all, had he not wanted to protect his son and teach him a salutary survival lesson, Chapel might well not have been located and thus would have lived. Immediately following this information, we are given the reaction at the time of Mr Whitechapel to this awful turn of events. As a man who prides himself on his humane treatment of his slaves, he finds himself sorely discomforted. He ultimately looks for divine assistance in restoring his plantation to good order.

At this point, D'Aguiar introduces another complication into the storyline — namely the rape of Cook by Sanders Senior and thus the procreation of Chapel. We firstly ascertain this from his diary ramblings of guilty self-admission, and then learn of the impact upon defenceless Cook. Even more than this, we come to appreciate the loyal love and admiration that Cook feels for the aged Whitechapel, her ever-resolute husband and defender of her public good name. Chapel, the much-loved son of these two slaves, then presents his assessment of them and their views. His inability to be obedient to his father is obvious, as is the impact of his literacy and the Shakespearean account of the two forbidden lovers, Romeo and Juliet. Next we hear the cynical reaction of the Plantation Owners to the tragic death of Chapel and the public response of his father. This is juxtaposed with the poetic and idealised account of the world that Chapel conceives. The plantation owners are 'hard-nosed' and practical, and can only see their slaves to be 'stock', a far cry from the reflective sensitivity of Chapel's verses.

Chapters 7 to 10 refocus our attention upon the emerging relationship between Lydia and Chapel. Her well-intentioned desire to help the young Chapel entwines them in a maze of complicated emotions and brings them into conflict with both their parents and society. They come to rely upon dreams of a life together, as their intellectual attachment and mutual love of literature turns to physical desire. Cook, in chapter 8, secretly observes Chapel reading to Lydia, and is startled, yet vows to temporarily keep his secret from her husband whom she knows would strongly disapprove.

In chapter 11, the editor of *The Virginian* belittles Lydia and Chapel's vision of an egalitarian society eventuating in the South, thus acting at this point in the narrative to confront their dreams with hard reality.

We are presented with a different voice from the slave sector in chapter 12, namely that of Whitechapel's great granddaughter. She dreams of Africa and desperately wants her aged relative to acquaint her with her African roots. Yet he resists this since he has tried to deny his past links in pragmatically coming to terms with his station as a slave in another country. She wonders at his willingness to have told Sanders Junior of the whereabouts of Chapel. Finally, she discovers the inert and now dead body of the man she refuses to call 'Great' Grandfather. This provides the link with the final chapter, in which the murderer of Chapel (ironically his own half-brother) also discovers the Whitechapel's body, concluding, 'If you were white I would have wanted you as my father' (p. 134).

Forgetting becomes a completely understandable process for old Whitechapel. The reader can now appreciate how the system of slavery could lead to such brutal beatings and how someone could come to believe that obedience was a better way than rebellion. His acute suffering is expressed in his realisation that 'what's done...cannot now be undone, only understood' (p. 137). He now questions whether whites can continue to enforce slavery: '...how long can the master's daylight continue to rule our nights?' (p. 137). Ironically, only on his deathbed does he show the kind of thinking that will release others from their mental and physical enslavement on the Southern plantations.

Chronology of Main Events

Given D'Aguiar's episodic and 'chain-of-voices' style, there is an almost constant shift in time sequences in this novel. We therefore need to be clear about the true chronological sequencing of events. What follows is a dating of key events, and a listing of them in the order that they actually occurred rather than the pattern presented by the chapters.

Approximately 1711: Whitechapel enslaved in Africa (aged 10).

August 1st, 1790: Birth of Sanders Junior (and likely death of his mother).

1795: Birth of Lydia.

December 24th, 1796 (Christmas Eve): First rape of Cook by Sanders Senior; Chapel is conceived.

January 1st, 1797 (New Year's Day): Marriage of Cook and Whitechapel.

January 9th, 1797: Second (final) rape of Cook by Sanders Senior.

January 10th, 1797: Sanders Senior confronted by Mr Whitechapel over his abuse of Cook and obliged to apologise to both parties.

September 1st, 1798: Birth of Chapel.

March 3, 1810: editorial in *The Virginian* refers to the 'just and fair' punishment to a runaway slave of 200 lashes.

May–June 1810: Lydia (aged 15) writes to the editor of *The Virginian* and enters into several extended dialogues with him.

May 19th, 1810: The editor of *The Virginian* acknowledges receipt of a letter from a 'literate slave'; perhaps even a young Chapel?

Late June 1810: Cook dies of fever.

Late June 1810 (the day after his mother's death): Chapel runs away and subsequently dies (aged 12) as a result of the 200 lashes administered to him by his half-brother, Sanders Junior; editorial of June 30th refers to this specific incident and to its context.

Approximately 1811: Whitechapel dies, and is found by his Great Granddaughter and Sanders Junior who decides to take responsibility for burying him.

Language and Style

To convey the sense of multiple narration, D'Aguiar presents different chapters in different styles. He uses different forms of language, each one clearly associated with particular characters. This reinforces the idea that history and memory arise from the experiences and perceptions of different individuals. D'Aguiar himself has remarked, '...history is full of contradictions, and those contradictions are best shown by voices contradicting each other.'[3]

Old Whitechapel speaks as a man who has lived a long and often difficult life, having realised that experience is a powerful mechanism for learning and survival. Interestingly, D'Aguiar has not tried to emulate the actual speech patterns of such a man at this time, presumably because this would have parodied him and reduced the element of nobility which is central to his character. Whitechapel often speaks somewhat haltingly, given the pain that he has experienced in life, particularly from the sense of complicity he feels over the tragic death of his much-loved adopted son, Chapel. Yet he still speaks with a poetic touch, reflecting the undeniable sensitivity of this much-wronged old man.

By contrast, Mr Whitechapel speaks with a clear sense of the rational and logical. He is authoritative, direct and clear in his mode of speech: 'You, Whitechapel, agreed with me to contain your son's anarchic spirit. Whitechapel you failed. I trusted you and you disappointed me' (p. 28). He speaks openly to both his most senior slave and overseer, suggesting a characteristic sense of humanity about the man.

Sanders Senior, the man who sexually assaults Cook, finds it very difficult to express or to articulate his feelings. As a result, his account is presented

3 Metcalf, p. 1.

as personal diary entries, partially to explain his attacks upon a defenceless young black girl and to reveal his inability to speak openly to his own son.

Cook speaks with a full emotionalism and yet in a direct and open manner. Her sentences tend to be relatively short and uncomplicated, reflecting her lack of formal education since she has learnt directly through life experiences.

Chapel, in direct contrast to others, speaks in verse form, revealing his poetic and reflective sensitivities. He analyses that which surrounds him with a sense of the astute critic, yet he retains an idealised perception of his world in some ways. He therefore refuses to adopt the pragmatism that is his father's hallmark.

The plantation owners communicate with a sense of conceit and self-assurance about their own dominance over their world and their use of slaves to amass their wealth. Through their conversing with Mr Whitechapel, we come to appreciate their ridicule of his libertarian attitudes towards his slaves, and his apparent hypocrisy concerning the death of Chapel, a troublesome slave.

Lydia reflects openly and emotionally on her emerging love for 'her' Chapel. Her accounts are earnest and intensely personal, revealing the extent to which she finds herself torn between her duty as the daughter of a plantation owner and the growing and insistent love she feels for the forbidden Chapel. She challenges the prevailing attitudes towards slaves in a rational and reasoned manner through her correspondence with the editor of *The Virginian*.

The Virginian uses a distinctive style of the editorial, which enables us to gain a clear understanding of the prevailing ethics and morals of the whites of the day, and the logic employed to justify their treatment of blacks and women in the Southern States.

'Remembering' and 'Forgetting' are like 'bookends' supporting the contents and ideas contained in the novel. They encapsulate the impact of the main crises of the novel upon the centenarian Whitechapel as he attempts to deal with the emotional pain that engulfs him as he confronts the death of Chapel and his overwhelming sense of complicity.

Remembering (pp.1-2)

The novel opens with the resounding voice of the main protagonist, Whitechapel, recollecting his all-too painful memory of 'the whipping of a boy who had to know better somehow and would have learned with a good talking to...but not this, not this' (p. 2). Initially, he attempts to suppress the rising flood of memory, 'Don't make me remember. I forget as hard as I can' (p. 2).

Important Points

This compact two-page beginning confronts us directly with what could be a recurring theme for slaves: 'The future is just more of the past waiting to happen' (p. 1). That sentence also expresses Whitechapel's personal sense of hopelessness, his grief and bitterness. He comments on the loss of identity in his role of slave — and indicates his mental enslavement. The theme of memory as pain is introduced immediately and its corollary, the importance of forgetting to enable survival in the face of trauma and extreme pain.

1. Whitechapel (pp. 3-27)

Here, in chapter 1, Whitechapel reflects back to that first horrific morning after the awful death of Chapel, when he '...faced the world for the first time as a nobody, nameless...' (p. 3). He perceives his legitimate identity within the world of the plantation to have died with Chapel and so loses his capacity to truly 'live' life, having taken on the look and sense of hopelessness of his dying son. 'Worry cut those paths in my face' (p. 7). He comes to accept the taunts of his own numerous relatives as he adopts the pained expression of his dying stepson to be aptly named 'Sour-face'.

'My face says life is sour. A life that was fresh to begin with but one left out too long turned to this: counting the hours that drag through the dark...' (p. 8). Now he can only await the death that has seems too long in coming, having buried two wives, many children and his only son.

He accepts the judgement of his relatives as a 'Judas', the betrayer of the son he allegedly loved with all his heart and would always protect. Despite this, he subsequently gave him up to the unrelenting Sanders Junior to be punished, wrongly believing this would save Chapel from his so-called 'wrong -headedness'. He comes to accept the rejection by his own direct relatives on the plantation, as he knowingly becomes the target of their verbal abuse and sarcasm. He feels that there is blood staining his guilt-ridden conscience and therefore believes that he deserves the punishment of his ostracism from his fellow blacks and the pain which now characterises his long life. Indeed, he yearns to forget and thus to escape his all too-powerful and long memory.

We are given an account of the death of his young second wife, Cook, Chapel's mother (pp. 10-11). He desperately wants to be reunited with her in death. Her poignant final words, 'Don't keep me waiting too long' (p. 11), still echo in his long memory. The harrowing events surrounding the flight, capture and death of Chapel (pp. 22-26) end in Whitechapel holding his dead son in his arms 'by dusk that same day' (p. 11). His agony is now twofold because he cannot embrace death since his dead wife will blame him for Chapel's premature death and he has caused his own son's death.

We next learn of the horrific thrashing to death of the headstrong young man, Chapel, whom Whitechapel came to know as his son, the account intercut with comments that reveal the old slave's obedience and willingness to accept the authority of his white 'superiors'. Despite his belief that 'a simple lesson in obedience was all that my boy required' (p. 12) based on his fear that runaways go to a heavenly paradise rather than an earthly one, we soon witness the consequences of his decision to reveal Chapel's whereabouts. Whitechapel's own horror at the brutality of the thrashing as well as his own shock and pain when Sanders Junior strikes him too (p. 23) reveal the error of judgement he has made, for Sanders Junior does not obey Mr Whitechapel's orders to hold the young runaway until his return. Instead, in a fury, Sanders shouts that he will make an example of Chapel, because:

> Not to punish him now in the appropriate way would be an

> outrage against this entire plantation. I am the overseer...I do not take orders from a nigger...I don't care if you are 100 years old. You are a slave. Now get out of my way…or I will strap you up next to your son and give you as many lashes for your insolence. (p. 24)

Whitechapel desperately sends his grandchild, 'a man close to my son's age' (p. 25), for the deputy overseer who can confirm Mr Whitechapel's orders, but in vain. Whitechapel is humiliatingly restrained, forced to witness the 'public display of savagery' (p. 25) as his son is beaten almost to death with 200 lashes. The chapter then ends with Whitechapel revealing his complete loss of dignity and status, his extremely bitter realisation that he has become a 'killer of children' (p.27). He craves death rather than this death-in-life of rejection and blame from everyone it seems.

His longevity has ensured that his 'memory is longer than time...I want to forget' (p. 26). He describes the deadening of his senses as he watches his own beloved son die in agony, and then leaves the narrative to a host of other implicated characters, each of whom provides another perspective on this boy's horrific death.

Key Events

This chapter is critical to our understanding of Chapel's death, the event that reverberates throughout the novel in various ways. Here, their graphic re-telling through Whitechapel's memory heightens our awareness of Whitechapel's own agony — his misguided part in the affair and his naive trust of white authorities. We also receive the first account of Cook's death; an event that will be told from a number of perspectives as the novel unfolds. We witness too how easily things can escalate on a plantation with Chapel's beating — important later to our understanding of Mr Whitechapel's rather precarious position with other plantation owners.

Key Attitudes

The 'slave mentality' of obedience that has led to Whitechapel's long life is evident in:

- His acceptance of the master's view that his young wife's 'time had come and not everyone was able to become an old ox like me' (p. 14)
- His betrayal of his son's whereabouts

- His belief in two types of slaves — 'the slave who must experience everything for himself before coming to an understanding of anything and he who learns through observation.' (p. 14)
- His expectation that the overseer will wait for the master's return before punishing Chapel.

We also witness the brutality of white authorities in Sanders' behaviour and the absolute powerlessness of someone so obviously respected as Whitechapel. Prevailing white attitudes are clearly shown in Sanders' reasons for whipping Chapel.

Finally, we can understand Whitechapel's suffering as he speaks directly to us so honestly and so despairingly about his spiritual torment following Chapel's death.

Key Themes and Issues

- The pain of memory and the desire to forget
- The complete authority of whites over black slaves and the ultimate powerlessness of slaves regardless of status
- Compliance versus rebellion — the dilemma for slaves, evident in Whitechapel's belief that rebellion courts death, something Chapel will challenge, and that compliance is preferable. This issue becomes increasingly important; by the end of the novel we will see that even Whitechapel can question the continuation of slavery (see p. 137).

2. Mr Whitechapel (pp. 28–35)

Next we hear the voice of the master, Mr Whitechapel, the owner of the plantation and all its slaves.

Immediately following the death of Chapel, he calls the three men together whom he holds accountable for what he perceives to be a blight upon his reputation as a compassionate and humane plantation owner. It also offends his sense of Christianity (revealed in the heated discussion he has with his colleagues in chapter 6). So, Whitechapel, Sanders Junior (the head slave overseer) and the unnamed deputy overseer are summonsed to his dining room to be admonished for failing to observe his specific orders to hold Chapel in his absence. He has been away briefly in the North where he took his wife and cherished daughter, Lydia.

Significantly, he speaks first to his most senior slave on the plantation, in entirely reasonable terms, much as a ruler might speak to a subject or even to a close friend:

> Your son's death is a matter of deepest regret to us all...You should have saved him from himself, Whitechapel...Close the door behind you like a good man. (p. 29)

Attitude to Sanders Junior

Whilst both of his two white employees are admonished for their failure to obey orders, it is Sanders Junior who incurs most of the wrath of his employer. He especially reminds him of the generational links which exist between the two of them, their dead fathers, and Whitechapel. He uses a repeated analogy, 'What began as a single thread has...woven itself into a prodigious carpet that cannot be unwoven' (p. 33). He speaks to his two employees in a scathing and uncompromising manner, reserving his harshest criticism for his most senior man, Sanders Junior (here called Sanders), threatening, 'Tell me why I should retain you when I can't trust you not to ruin me?'(p. 30). He then proceeds to admonish him for maltreating Whitechapel, observing 'he deserved better treatment' (p. 31). He reminds him that Whitechapel is a living link with their own fathers, almost implying a blood link. After alluding to what he deems to be the appropriate treatment of slaves, he states, '...there is simply too much history between us all to justify what you did last night' (p. 33).

Sanders Junior's True Relationship to Chapel

Then, unwittingly, he reveals to Sanders Junior that in killing the young black runaway slave, Chapel, supposedly the only son of the centenarian Whitechapel, he has also in reality killed his own half-brother. 'Your father was supposed to inform you and that was the end of it. No one was to raise the matter ever again' (p. 34). He reveals the extent of the tragedy and inhumanity of Chapel's death; that Sanders has the same biological father and that he is also inextricably connected to Whitechapel, who had essentially covered up the moral indignity of Cook's rape and the true paternity of her child. Interestingly, he reminds him also that 'Whitechapel's longevity and living memory...' (p. 35) ultimately ensure that the sins of the past are not forgotten, nor are their consciences allowed to remain at ease because of his presence. Tragedy it seems has befallen all of them in some manner or other.

Mr Whitechapel's Authority

The tone of his speech reflects his judgement of the trio: Whitechapel he remonstrates with in a reasoned manner that belies the power relationship that exists between them. In this way he seeks to secure his ongoing support, ensuring that the other plantation slaves continue to be essentially compliant. The close of his monologue to Whitechapel signifies this: 'Close the door behind you like a good man' (p. 29).

Reasonableness and Humanity

Chapter 2 links with the former by presenting us with the voice of the 'Master', the man who controls the fate of his numerous slaves and who believes that he is an enlightened and humane slave owner — something of a contradiction in terms. He says that slaves should be treated 'first and foremost as subjects of God', something he qualifies by admitting that they are, though, '...blessed with lesser faculties, and therefore suited to the trade of slavery' (p. 32).

Nevertheless, we gain an insight into the moral precepts by which Mr Whitechapel, as a 'liberal' slave owner, lives and operates. Yet, despite this, he is still unarguably a man who relies upon the forced labour of other humans obliged to work to maintain his opulent lifestyle. His fellow plantation owners in chapter 6 astutely refer to this point.

Memory

Mr Whitechapel here emphasises the importance of the past to present relationships, stressing that everyone is interlinked through these events. Memory is the key that enables individuals to take that past into account in their present behaviour.

3. Sanders Senior (pp. 36–53)

Over a period of almost two years, we trace the inner voice of this callous white overseer, who worked for Mr Whitechapel's father, part of the initial thread of the carpet to which Mr Whitechapel refers.

The perpetrator of an earlier horror, Sanders Senior, now speaks via a set of personal diary entries which trace his growing sense of loneliness and sexual frustration following the untimely death of his wife, Caroline, who presumably died giving birth to his only son, Sanders Junior. He, like Whitechapel, is haunted by the memory of his beloved wife and by his inability to tell his young son the truth about her fate. He then becomes irritated by his son's interest in Whitechapel, who 'is by far the best worker, and...has the most agreeable manner' (p.37).

His Relationship with Cook

However, it is the arrival of a new black cook that is by far the most momentous event for this unsettled man. This young, nubile, attractive and competent black cook re-awakens his latent sexual urges and soon he fantasises about having a sexual encounter with her, along with a group of other white women. Meanwhile, the realisation that Whitechapel intends to marry Cook angers and irritates Sanders Senior. Whitechapel may be '...kind, the best of the plantation stock' (p. 41), but Sanders Senior resents his impending marriage to this highly desirable young woman, and accordingly engineers its postponement. His sexual obsession with Cook rapidly grows. Finally, on Christmas Eve, he grabs and rapes Cook in his marital bed, offering her the recompense of 'whatever she wanted from [his] wife's closet in return for her silence' (p. 45). Her morally indignant response is to demand the right to marry Whitechapel straight away, given that Sanders Senior had been thwarting and delaying this until then.

The marriage of Cook and Whitechapel takes place on New Year's Day. Sanders Senior once more attacks and rapes the vulnerable Cook, some eight days later. This time, just as in the case of his son's admonitions by Mr Whitechapel years later, Sanders Senior finds his own position on the plantation in question. He ponders, 'The word of a white man is worth that of how many slaves?' (p. 46) reminding us of the irony of his circumstances from the point of view of slaves.

Sanders' Punishment

He is issued with a set of unpalatable punishments: a hefty monetary fine; forced apologies to not only Cook but also Whitechapel; and, the final insult, obligatory marriage to a 'toothless, palsied hag' (p. 51). Perhaps the ultimate ignominy remains the realisation that he is the secret father of the boy Cook gives birth to, one he will obviously encounter in his duties around the plantation.

His Attitude towards Slaves

We also become aware that his treatment of slaves is quite different from the Master's. When Sanders Senior also deals with a runaway slave, he punishes him with some 200 lashes, which results in his untimely death; ironically this is the same as in the case of Chapel some 13 years later at the hands of Sanders' own son, who is, of course, also Chapel's half-brother. We hear the inner voice of this man who is such a hardened and unyielding man in public, who has no sense of generosity towards slaves, unlike his employer who thinks him 'too severe with them' (p. 37).

Sanders' Emotional State

The side of this man's character we access here is the emotionally and sexually bereft man, left only with a young son to remind him of the dead wife for whom he so longs. The first rape of Cook, one might speculate, is, in part, a statement of power over the hapless and 'noble' Whitechapel. Cook's refusal of his offer of her choice of his dead wife's clothes in return for her silence, shows her dignity remains intact even if her chastity does not.

Mr Whitechapel's Anxiety

The fact that all are sworn to secrecy indicates the power Mr Whitechapel wields: in this way he shows his anxiety to ensure publicly the continued good moral reputation of his plantation; one might argue, a logical inconsistency for a slave plantation!

4. Cook (pp. 54–55)

D'Aguiar then allows us to hear the voice of the much wronged Cook in the shortest of all 13 chapters. Here we enter the mind of a simple, illiterate young black woman, who ironically counts herself as being blessed to have such a husband as 'my Whitechapel' (p.55). Following her rapes, she contemplates suicide, but is 'saved' by Whitechapel whose influence with their master ensures that Sanders Senior is truly punished and that some sense of justice prevails in a world where there is so little for slaves. She acknowledges her own folly at initially mocking Whitechapel's interest in her, now realising that, 'He can love. He proves he loves me every day' (p. 55). She concludes that she wants to bear many sons for him, and when he is dead, 'grow old with my sons, alone, and happy to have met my Whitechapel' (p. 55).

Important Points

Importantly, Cook's first narrative directly follows the journal entries of her white attacker. It is written in the style of an open interviewee, with an openness and directness that immediately strikes the reader; here is an uneducated woman laying before us the facts of the matter and her appraisal of them. This, then, is not filtered memory, it is truth, almost as told to a policewoman by such a rape victim. She totally owes her life to the forgiving spirit of Whitechapel. So, chapter 4, the shortest of all the chapters, becomes a proclamation of boundless love. Despite her hideous abuse, the powerful healing element of love is evident. This is almost an idyll after the horror she has experienced.

5. Chapel (pp. 56–64)

Chapter 5 is the only one to provide us with the voice of Chapel, written in the reflective and idealistic form of poetry. Poetry is also the classic means of entering the human soul, speaking as it does through its condensed and compressed language.

Chapel longs to be a professional writer and poet, and together with Lydia, looks idealistically towards a new social order free from racism or slavery.

This chapter is written after her father caught him and Lydia alone in the plantation mansion, when Chapel was reading from a Shakespeare classic tale of forbidden love:

> I must have got lost in the image of her
> Or the story of two star-crossed lovers (p. 60)

Chapel reflects upon his father's treatment of him, his mother's redoubtable virtues and his boundless love for her. Then he refers to 'my other schooling' (p. 59), namely Lydia patiently teaching him to read and write, entreating him 'not to tell a soul' (p. 60). The account ends with the Master's words echoing in Chapel's memory, threatening him with dire consequences should he ever catch him reading again or in Lydia's presence. Now he and Lydia must resort to clandestine meetings, where they 'speak from memory' (p. 62): he composing loving poems for her and she exchanging memorised tracts of literary classics in return.

Their romance is based upon memory, dreams and heady idealism. He finally cannot accept his father's advice about being the right type of slave, 'shaking [his] head at the abyss / Between [them]' (p.64). Consequently, he resolves that without Lydia or his now dead mother, he has to leave.

> With her gone nothing could keep me there.
> Father, I am running. I feel joy; not fear (p. 64).

The reasons for Chapel's fateful flight from the Whitechapel Plantation are stated, and we can better understand the desperation of his attempt to gain his liberty.

6. Plantation Owners (pp. 65–78)

The tragic events that form the nucleus of this saga are then analysed in a chapter that reveals the inherent tension that exists between Mr Whitechapel and his plantation-owning colleagues.

This chapter gives an account of the events connected with Mr Whitechapel's visit to his exclusive Club on a symbolically black and wet night. D'Aguiar has chosen to use a multi-layered approach to dialogue here, using italics to capture the inner voice of Mr Whitechapel, with all its anxiety and fear of peer critique, followed by the frenzied dialogue which ensues between him and his very vocal plantation-owning critics.

They seek to label him a hypocrite following news of Chapel's death after whipping as this flies in the face of his avowed humane treatment of his slaves. They try to reinstate his comradeship with them by emphasising his decisive and brutal treatment of this one slave. He rejects their insults, for which they label him a traitor of the worst kind in their eyes — that of an abolitionist. He reaffirms his Christian beliefs, upholding his own-avowed morally righteous position. He echoes Lydia's suggestion to the editor of *The Virginian* (p. 114) in perhaps even liberating and paying slaves to access their labour, which produces exclamations of astonishment. He then recounts the extraordinary events surrounding Chapel's whipping by his half-brother, using the same image of the thread woven through time as he does in admonishing the perpetrator, Sanders Junior (p. 33). He, like Sanders Senior, refers once more to the nobility of Whitechapel, whose loyalty to the plantation produces exclamations: 'That slave of yours is a slaver's dream' (p. 77). Mr Whitechapel feels restored to public and private dignity at the end — clearly through the actions of the ever-loyal Whitechapel.

7. Lydia; 8. Cook; 9. & 10 Lydia (pp. 79–103)

Chapters 7 to 10 to a large extent explore the crucial, yet doomed, link between Lydia and Chapel.

Lydia's maturation and growing realisation that she has fallen in love with one of her father's unattainable black slaves (albeit a young man of mixed race in reality!) is revealed. She goes from being Chapel's 'big sister' (p. 79), to being his 'darling', who, she dreams, '...will write verses and make our lives and the lives of our children rich' (p. 103).

Cook's Reactions to Chapel's Literacy

Wedged in between these accounts of the maturing Lydia, we again hear the simple and straightforward voice of Cook. In chapter 8, she begins to realise that her own beloved son is learning to read from the equally cherished daughter of her Master's House, and fears the potential consequences of this, especially when Sanders Junior was expressly forbidden from fraternising with 'Miss Lydia' as he was seen to be too much of a 'distraction'. Yet, she is also understandably proud of this remarkable achievement of her own son: 'My son can open a book and sound like the master' (p. 85). She also recognises its potential power. She resolves not to tell her own husband, because he would want to stop Chapel from reading, based upon his own life of obedience, '...as an example of the slave who has done all the proper things to survive and earn the respect of the master and overseer' (p. 86). Yet she decides that 'What I heard must not be taken from him' (p. 86). She compensates for this by making the cooking pot sweeter than usual.

Lydia and Chapel's Love

Lydia's growing infatuation with her Chapel is put to the test by their forced secret meetings (just like the hapless Romeo and Juliet), and by her parents' increasing determination that she marry and take her rightful place in Southern white plantation society. Now her beloved volumes of literary classics by Shakespeare and Milton are to be used on her head for improved deportment, rather than for the improvement of her intellect. She finally becomes a loving and yearning, headstrong young woman. She endeavours to create a way for them to be more than idealised 'star- crossed lovers', perceiving the liberated North to provide the two of them with a possibility for long-term happiness. However, we perceive that her final notions of their future together, with 'Chapel...writing verses for a living' (p. 103), represent a fanciful and decidedly impractical idea.

11. *The Virginian* (pp. 104–121)

Chapter 11 sees D'Aguiar using yet another form of narrative — seventeen editorials from the fictitious influential white paper, The Virginian, *published over some six months in 1809–1810. Each one of these directly or indirectly interrelates with the events of the novel, including several interchanges between the editor and Lydia, a letter from Chapel to the editor*

> *and one from the Whitechapel Plantation Deputy Overseer. It also becomes the vehicle for both Lydia and Chapel to engage in indirect debates about the rights of slaves to both read and write and to be treated as paid labourers as well as potential marital partners.*

Each of the editorials centres on an element of the treatment of slaves within white Virginian plantation society, thus revealing the predominant concerns of these white male slave owners. Accordingly, echoes of the voice of the editor are to be found in the words of Mr Whitechapel, especially in chapter six with its interchanges with other plantation owners. Issues addressed include:

- The question of compatibility between whipping slaves and remaining a true Christian
- The correct protocols with respect to buying and selling slaves — '...the degree of humanity [they] should accord slaves...' (p. 106)
- The appropriate punishment for runaway slaves; the way to treat '...the very old slave who has given a life of good service but who is now too old to be of much use' (p.109)
- The 'temptation' posed by 'young, nubile female slaves'
- The coexistence of slavery and Christianity
- The running of the plantation and its treatment of slaves
- The perceived long-term future of slavery
- The payment of wages to freed slaves in return for their willing provision of labour rather than forced slavery
- The impact of literacy upon slaves
- Whether poor whites are worse off than plantation owners or even slaves themselves
- Finally — and most significantly given both the implications for the plot here and for white Southern society in general — the morality of 'liaisons' between white women and black men.

Racism

Through all of these, we encounter fundamental challenges to the prevailing racist orthodoxy of the day, and the ostensibly logical replies of the editor. In essence then, we hear a white commentary on these circumstances and perceive just how long it will take for a Lydia and a

Chapel to be able to live openly and with social acceptance in the Deep South.

12. Great Granddaughter (pp. 122-128)

There is an apparent discrepancy between the title of this chapter here — 'Great Grandmother' — and that in the Contents page — 'Great Granddaughter', one which D'Aguiar himself originally intended, perhaps to present yet another sense of the lasting impact of memory. Since publication, he has indicated that he has rethought this inconsistency and now wants the chapter to be uniformly seen to be the voice of Whitechapel's Great Granddaughter.

Chapter 12 allows us to hear the voice of one of Whitechapel's young descendants, one of his Great Granddaughters. She reflects upon her Great Grandfather's African roots and his memories of his early childhood — yet another set of powerful memories he seems to carry with him through his long life. We learn of the way in which Whitechapel was captured as a young ten-year-old boy in his native Africa (p. 122) and realise that he has been a slave for the better part of 90 years! She enters the world of his past in Africa through her dreams and tries to connect with his roots. She acknowledges her own origins through this dreaming, whilst Whitechapel tells her to 'make her dreams' in her own real world and not to hanker for an unattainable existence. This is similar to his pragmatic advice to his own son about the wise behaviour for a slave. Her dreams have been halted by the hideous reality of the beating of Chapel, and she sees how, because 'the whip exacted as much of a toll on his aged body as his son's' that she 'could do nothing for him' (p.127) from the day of Chapel's death.

After the horrific beating and subsequent death of Chapel, Great Grandfather became 'a ghost we all see and ignore because he killed his only son' (p.126). For his great granddaughter too 'he shrank in stature before [her] eyes' (p. 127). Before his death she longs to ask him 'what form of reasoning could have convinced [him] that his son would be safe?' (p. 128) and hear his answer because to her he is infallible. However, this never happens. Instead, she now must try to wash the truly dead body of this same 'Great' Grandfather, but she 'cannot carry on' (p. 128), her feelings for him being simply too strong.

13. Sanders Junior (pp. 129-134)

The final numbered chapter shows Sanders Junior, the cause of Chapel's death (his undiscovered half-brother) and, indirectly also Whitechapel's, trying to deal appropriately with the corpse of the dead Whitechapel. He now regrets that he dishonourably struck Whitechapel during the lashing of his son. He recognises the centrality of Whitechapel to the smooth running of the plantation when he admits that 'You were a better overseer than I' (p. 130). He wonders why Chapel was so different in spirit and manner. He even admires the childlike way in which Whitechapel lies and vows to give him a proper marked grave. He also notes that the master will perceive it to be a potentially bad omen for the whole plantation and so will react 'badly' to the news of the death of the elder statesman of his slaves. He realises that he is like his father, Sanders Senior, but cannot fully admire him the way he does Whitechapel. Dramatically, he pronounces 'If you were white I would have wanted you as my father' (p. 134).

Forgetting

In 'Forgetting', we return to Whitechapel's thoughts even though we now know he has died.

Whitechapel imagines what he ought to say to his son, and laments the inadequacy he perceives in himself as a father. He recognises that Chapel pursued his dreams, that Lydia was part of this dreaming, and yet, as a person of mixed race, maybe he was entitled to yearn for the seemingly unattainable. He wonders what the real future of slavery is, understanding the mutual dependency created by the entire system of slavery between master and dutiful slave, yet also sensing change when he ponders: ' But how long can the master's daylight continue to rule our nights?' (p. 137)

As death creeps up on him, his sour mouth tastes a new type of sourness. At last, it seems the hapless old man, the ever-loyal and compliant black slave is granted his oft-repeated wish by being released from the memories that haunt him in this life. Thus, the end of the novel gives us a sense of resolution for the key protagonist, Whitechapel, as he seems free at last from the multiple pains he has endured during his long life. Even with his death though, the memories of his existence and the tragedy connected with Chapel remain firmly implanted in the hearts and minds of all on the plantation.

Importance of Context

One needs to be mindful of the extent to which the Whitechapel Plantation in so many respects forms the outer boundaries of the lives of these people. After all, this is a very insular existence, largely self-contained; especially given the ostracism the Deep South receives from the anti-slave North at this time. In addition, we need to acknowledge the lack of contact possible with the outside world, with limited communication and information typically being gleaned from the likes of the biased and selective pages of *The Virginian*. This then is a world more heavily influenced by tradition and heredity than by change and development. People here are often limited in their relationships by the actions or reputations of their parents, and assumptions are made about individuals based upon their forebears. One indication of this is apparent when the plantation owner angrily reminds his young overseer, the son of the previous one: 'There is simply too much history between us all to justify what you did...' (p. 33). As a result, these characters are closely interrelated and interconnected, often manifesting in-bred attitudes. The society too is largely closed and its structures apparently unchanging.

Whitechapel

The aged figure of the ever-loyal black slave, Whitechapel, is so named as a mark of respect by Mr Whitechapel's father, the first plantation owner. Ironically, his name also indicates that he is owned, a slave to the essential work of the plantation. Whitechapel is central to the plot as well as to the entire fabric of the novel. His voice opens and closes the text in a curiously detached and controlled manner given the horrors he has witnessed and experienced. Here is a man who is almost a walking history book, a veritable piece of 'living memory', whose absolute reliability and loyalty to his slave master is redoubtable, as even the other plantation owners recognise, 'Name your price. That slave of yours is a slaver's dream' (p. 77).

However, his long life has also meant he is enveloped by a host of memories, too many of which are now painful, and yet unavoidable it seems: 'Memory hurts...Don't make me remember. I forget as hard as I can.' (p. 2) 'Memory is pain trying to resurrect itself.' (p. 138)

His greatest pain relates to the son he adopted whose death haunts him. He feels the weight of culpability, given that his revelation to the master of Chapel's whereabouts (done because he thought it would teach Chapel a lesson) brings about Chapel's horrific and gruesome public murder. Once he is forced to witness the gruesome death of his beloved and headstrong thirteen-year-old son, Whitechapel dies an inner death, signified by his feeling that he is not worthy to have a name — he is not even worthy enough to be a slave. In D'Aguiar's words, 'he erases himself through namelessness'.[4]

His longevity, then, has ironically not been a blessing but rather a curse. Here is a man who realises now that he has survived in spite of (and not because of) his status as a slave. He has indeed outlived so many of those around him, including the old plantation owner who named him after himself, and the old overseer who raped his cherished second young wife, always observing the dictum that he presents to his beloved only son — learn through the mistakes and experiences of others. He believes that it is important to be consistent, obedient, unchanging, and conciliatory — to keep things calm. However, Whitechapel himself has not acquired the contentment or calm that he knows should accompany his status as the 'elder statesman' of the plantation slaves. Like Macbeth, he can only perceive death to be a release from this somewhat illogical world where life: '...is a tale/Told by an idiot, full of sound and fury/ Signifying nothing' (Act 5, sc. 5, lines 26-29).

He ultimately seems to be a victim of the same system to which he has been so absolutely loyal. This reminds us that, under such a system of slavery that Whitechapel endures, there can be no real justice, reason or fairness. The trusted slave, even in such a liberal plantation as this one, is still a human being denied his fundamental rights by other human beings; this can only end in misery and, in Whitechapel's case, tragedy. Why, we might well ask, has this aged black man so long adhered to his principle of compliance when to have broken out of this mould might have produced a vestige of happiness and hope for such a loyal man. Indeed, it is his loyalty to both the master, Mr Whitechapel, and to his own principles of action as a supposed 'wise slave', that spells the doom of his only son, and ultimately saps his own will to live.

Ironically, even though he is working on a more humane plantation than those around, as evident in the voices of other plantation owners, he still

---

4 Metcalf, p. 6

suffers. The injustices of the system become apparent when someone reasonable like Whitechapel misjudges the power of the overseer and also the impact of 200 lashes! Perhaps the main feeling we develop here is one of anger and frustration at the enormous sense of loss in the unrealised potential observable in this amazing and dignified centenarian. We cannot delude ourselves that this plantation has been 'good' to him — or indeed — that he has in any sense been fortunate to have lived for so long. A further irony is evident. Despite his admirable principles, in the long run Whitechapel is the kind of slave who perpetuates slavery because he does not question its basic injustices. We see at the very end that he realises that slavery cannot continue — so, although he does not become an agent of change, as more radical slaves such as Chapel will, he does understand the need for change. Others, though, will have to fight that battle.

Chapel

Physically and spiritually, Chapel, as the progeny of a black mother and a white father, represents a meeting of the races that are divided so absolutely by both the written laws and social conventions of the Deep South. Somewhat ironically, as the social son of the black slave elder statesman of the Whitechapel Plantation and his consequently important wife, the main house's Cook, he is given access to those elements of white society that have long been so forbidden to blacks — books.

It is not merely his capacity to read and write which are so significant in themselves, but rather his capacity to read great works of literature, with all their insights into human behaviour and morality. He is also able to articulate his hopes and dreams through that most potent and concentrated emotional form of self-expression — poetry. D'Aguiar also states that he used poetry to show that Chapel was 'clearly schooled'.[5]

Poetry not only reflects reality but also evokes Chapel's youthful dreaming and longing for a better world. In Chapel, we surely see, a sense of hope for a new age of equality arising out of the best elements of civilisation rather than out of a desire for revenge, even though revenge is perhaps more understandable. We are reminded of the same voice of reason that was echoed in the very well publicised words of both Nelson Mandela and Archbishop Desmond Tutu in South Africa. They somehow averted the widely-expected racial bloodbath from occurring after white rule

5 Metcalf, p. 2

and the evils of apartheid ended in that country in the early 1990s after over a century of existence.

Chapel's love for Lydia is, in the first instance, based upon a mutual love of literature. This is clearly a meeting of the minds and souls, a pole apart from the animal lust which saw Chapel's conception through the brutal rape of Cook by the obsessed Sanders Senior. In the rarefied atmosphere of the main house's library — so much at odds with both the reality of the brutal cotton fields outside and the primitive conditions to which the black slaves are subjected — they are cocooned by their love of the language and lure of the ideas of great canons of literature.

Whilst his mother may sense pride at Chapel 'sound[ing] like the master' (p. 85), Lydia also becomes besotted with his presence and his reading voice: 'At what point do I stop hearing the words and listen to the voice alone and realise I am in love with its cadence?' (p. 87) When forbidden to meet, they rely on memory to continue their 'reading' — he relating his poems and she tracts from literary works. Unlike Whitechapel for whom memory is a great burden, it becomes the means which perpetuates their happiness, albeit restricted and dangerous.

They are both drawn to the image of Shakespeare's fateful star-crossed lovers, Romeo and Juliet, also forbidden young lovers of two sets of parents for whom such a union is utterly impossible and socially outrageous. Like Shakespeare's equally young lovers (around 13), Chapel (12) and Lydia (15) believe in the virtue of their own seemingly-fantastical love and see flight to another safe place — in this case, the more tolerant North — to be their one chance for true happiness.

Chapel's unwillingness to follow the advised behaviours of his father may be seen to be the inevitable generational gap, or perhaps it reflects the optimism of the dreamer. He is the non-compliant slave who in his father's eyes is doomed because disobedience and rebellion bring danger and death in their wake. Indeed, Chapel's death is horrific, totally unnecessary, potentially avoidable and tragic in the sense of loss and wasted potential. After all, here was a young man who had the capacity and literary skill, without the benefit of any formal schooling, to reflectively observe and comment on the world in which he found himself. He can also see a world that might have been and hence can be seen as a prospective visionary. He is the figure who points the way to changes ahead, but is historically caught in the insistence of the plantation owners that slavery is still an economic necessity in the Southern States.

Cook

This young woman's 'name' identifies only her role on the plantation; it signifies her slave status and Mr Whitechapel's ownership of her. As a very young woman she was brutally raped and assaulted by her then master, Sanders Senior. However, she retains a remarkable sense of hope for the future, in no small measure the result of the generous spirit and love she is given by her devoted husband, Whitechapel. This seems to be reinforced by the pride and sense of expectation she holds for her only son, Chapel.

Whilst she remains illiterate, she is only too well aware of the potential impact of literacy and its links with power: 'He sounds as if he is standing at a pulpit or like the master sounds when he says prayers to the whole plantation at Christmas' (p. 84). Her pride is boundless, it seems, at his capability. 'Chapel speaking, not from memory but lifting words from a book with his eyes. My Chapel' (p. 84). Nevertheless, she is also only too mindful of the dangers such ability may bring in its wake. 'Books will only bring you trouble. Books will only increase the number of things you have to worry about' (p. 86). This recognition of latent dangers of literacy is something the plantation owners readily acknowledge too. However, as a mother, who is so proud of her only son's significant achievement, she is not willing for either her husband or herself to chastise him for his skill.

Cook also reveals the lot of the female slave — subject not only to a system which denies her individual identity but also to the luck of the draw with a husband, as the plantation owner had the final say in whom the male slaves could marry. Her deep gratitude for Whitechapel's readiness to marry her and save her honour after she has been raped shows how aware she is that her life might have been lived with the brutal Sanders, a lot which might have befallen her without a Whitechapel and a more humane plantation owner.

She is particularly fortunate in being the plantation cook as her living conditions are much superior to the women who had to work in the fields. Her two cooking pots (p. 86) reveal the two standards she lives under, as we can be certain the superior food is for the master. Her death from fever, while it highlights how precarious life was for everyone in this period, leaves her husband and son both devastated and lonely without her gentle love and quiet wisdom.

Lydia

Lydia, the only daughter of the master of the plantation, plays a pivotal role in this narrative as she provides Chapel with his crucial literacy. She initiates the whole process, intentionally leaving the door of the reading room open, hoping to lure inside this young inquisitive black boy. When she sees his reaction to her reading, 'his face lights up' (p. 80), she resolves to teach him to read. He quickly acquires a basic proficiency, and she is caught up in his infectious delight at this newfound skill. Later, as he reads to her, she '...recline[s] in [her] chair and let[s] his voice cascade over [her] body' (p. 81).

Already, even though they are but children, it seems that a strong bond and affection is developing between them, clearly with absolutely no regard whatsoever for the gulf which lies between them because of their heredity, social circumstances or race. Lydia then resolves to teach him to write as well, so completing his literacy skills.

Chapter nine, the second of Lydia's three chapters, immediately follows the revelation that Cook is well aware of the skills Lydia has taught her beloved only son. Here, Lydia and Chapel are caught in the midst of their idyll — Chapel's reading of the beauty of Shakespeare's poetic language. She has just become aware of the change that has occurred over the two years in which their liaison has existed. Love has unwittingly replaced their former friendship as Lydia's 'body is suddenly hot' (p. 87). She fears especially for Chapel, realising that '...I love a boy three years my junior. I realize I am in love with a slave' (p. 88).

Lydia cannot accept her father's views concerning the supposedly 'gravest injustice' committed upon Chapel in giving him the capacity to read and write. Instead, she clearly recognises that, for it to be illegal for a slave to read and write is a deprivation that is truly 'unjust'. Her father's admonitions to her about the danger she will bring to herself and to their whole family are absolute as he bans any form of communication between them, noting that perhaps they will be able to be together, but not until the next century, that is, after death! Her inner reaction seems tinged with sarcasm, if not defiance: 'I understand, Father. I understand perfectly' (p. 88).

Meanwhile, Cook plants the strategy for defiance — the meetings in the dark at night (p. 89), where they become true 'star-cross'd lovers' it seems. Lydia acknowledges the irony that Chapel is far more proud of his slave father and his words of advice than she is of her father, the master.

Again the power of the memory motif is brought to bear here. Chapel asks Lydia to memorise one of their mutual literary delights for their next meeting — for it is absolutely clear that this will be but the first of many such nightly meetings — 'lover's trysts'. Lydia thinks in response, 'Chapel, I want to say, all my memory is yours' (pp. 90-91). We realise that Lydia wants to reclaim their happy times together, as well as impart her storehouse of literary gems. Neither of them is prepared to break her father's ruling, and like Romeo and Juliet, they pledge their love, albeit so apparently futile: 'We both know it cannot go on' (p. 91).

As Lydia matures into a woman (chapter 10), she remains preoccupied with thoughts of Chapel, whilst her parents become intent upon grooming her for her 'rightful place' in plantation society. Now the volumes of the literary greats such as Shakespeare, Milton and Spencer are to be used for her appropriate deportment as a Southern Belle and not for her intellectual advancement. As a white woman of social standing and status, she is expected to conform to the conventions of society, where a woman is but another chattel for a well-to-do young man. Lydia is being groomed to become a virtual slave to her husband's desires and expectations. Lydia finds the string of white suitors decidedly unappealing. 'I hold each of these men up beside Chapel to see how they compare. Not one has wit, intelligence, charm and sensitive nature. Not one.' (p. 93).

Her father gently tries to persuade her of the wisdom of marriage, but her mother is much blunter, more insistent. This leads Lydia to feel trapped and to further long for Chapel, and to wish that either he were white — or, she black; at last, she pointedly seems aware of the division their skin colour places between them. It is her brother Thomas' return from the relatively libertarian North that 'saves her', with images of inter-racial relationships, a vision of 'heaven on earth' that she conveys to Chapel at their next illicit meeting. Their meetings become increasingly physical and sensual, as their longing for each other constantly intensifies. It is the image of the North that sustains them, as Lydia tries to engineer a way for them to meet when she accompanies her brother and mother there. They dream of the life they see themselves enjoying there, based we see on very shaky and uncertain foundations, with Chapel supporting them by writing verses. Such an occupation naturally highlights the extent of his literary mastery, but it also reveals the impracticality and impossibility, one suspects, of their much-anticipated life together.

During the course of May and June, 1810, Lydia writes several letters to the editor of *The Virginian,* exploring alternative ways of treating and relating to slaves. In the first place, she explores the implications of slavery 'dying as an institution' (p. 115) and the possibility of hiring slaves as a paid workforce rather than a forced system of labour (p. 114). Along with her father, Lydia also corresponds concerning the desirability for slaves to be given literacy skills, maintaining that 'it would improve mankind' (p. 117). The editor is dismissive of her notions, putting them down to the 'unmitigated idealism' (p.117) of the young. The editor obviously perceives Lydia to be unrealistic and incapable of truly understanding the fundamental operation of the plantations. Yet, on the contrary, this correspondence on Lydia's part reveals not only her close analysis of the plantation system which surrounds her, and has trapped her beloved Chapel, but also suggests that she refuses to accept the Southern Belle facade laid before her by her mother in particular; she may balance the wisdom and insights of key literary works on her head, but she has not lost her capacity for reasoning as a consequence.

However, it is the correspondence concerning relationships between white women and black men, which shows not only Lydia's resolve, but also the extent of Southern antipathy towards such inter-racial relations. The editor's scathing reply and stinging rebuke to Lydia, sees such 'liaisons' to be '...practices that harm the smooth working of a country' (p. 121).

He concludes by attacking Lydia, noting that he had 'credited her...with intelligence' originally, but now perceives himself to have been 'grossly mistaken'. Her 'love for blacks', states the editor, 'clouds her ability to reason about any subject involving them' (p.121). This comment is heavily ironical because it is the editor who is so bigoted and steeped in his sense of racial superiority that he is unable to accept any treatment of blacks as fellow human beings.

Clearly then, Lydia's views and attitudes are threatening and utterly repugnant to the 'Establishment', that is, to the conservative elements in Southern society who were to be so instrumental in provoking the Civil War 50 years later. She is a non-conformist and a potential rebel, whose intellect, love for a black man and sense of justice all preclude an allegiance to a system such as this which is based upon a notion of racial supremacy.

Mr Whitechapel

Mr Whitechapel, despite being a slave-user and plantation owner entirely reliant upon the physical hard labour of his large contingent of slaves to maintain his fortune and lifestyle, is not an entirely unsympathetic character from our stance. Here is a man who is ridiculed by his peers for his lenient and relatively humane treatment of his slaves. Whilst we may find his attitudes towards Whitechapel, 'the most senior man on the plantation' (p. 28), to be rather condescending and patriarchal in the world of the 1990s, in the social context of this novel, he seems to be a reasonably good, straightforward and decent man.

Nevertheless, his attitudes seem to be borne of a sense of practicality and pragmatism, as he personally indicates to Whitechapel, 'My acquaintances tell me I am too lenient...No, I argue back...a satisfied slave is a happy slave and a more productive worker. Treat them like equals and they respond with nobility' (p. 29). At the very least, he acknowledges his slaves to be fellow human beings, capable of emotions and deserving of a degree of compassion.

When speaking to Whitechapel of the untimely and horrific death of his spirited son, Chapel, he speaks with some consideration, albeit contained: ' Your son's death is a matter of deepest regret to us all, but in our view he brought it upon himself' (p. 29). These are hardly the observations of a monster or an indifferent and callous man. Indeed, the terms in which he speaks to Whitechapel are remarkably open and direct, and are even delivered within the walls of the plantation mansion. Whilst he chastises Whitechapel, his strongest and harshest criticisms are reserved for his two senior white employees. His dismissal of Whitechapel is even in almost comradely terms, 'Close the door behind you like a good man.' (p. 29).

We of course have witnessed Mr Whitechapel's long-time respect as evidenced by his dealings with old Whitechapel after the rape of Cook and birth of Chapel and his comments to his peers at the Gentlemen's Club. It seems that for the Master, the existence of Whitechapel is living proof that his slaves are both contented and well treated, and that as a Christian, he is benevolent towards his slaves. So, presumably, Whitechapel's death will prove to be a severe psychological blow to Mr Whitechapel. Perhaps his death will signify not only the end of an era but also the end of the Whitechapel Plantation as we know it, especially given our realisation that Lydia will never be the compliant and dutiful daughter to fulfil the 'Southern Belle' role expected of her.

It is his reaction to the rape of Cook that most clearly reveals shows his own sense of morality and decency. He insists that Sanders Senior is penalised and no public sign of the events be shown, suggesting his belief in moral propriety and a total rejection of the common occurrence elsewhere of black female slaves falling prey to the sexual demands of white men. He wants his plantation to be a model of 'Christian virtue', within his prevailing notion of Christianity that includes the perception that black slaves are actually uncivilised heathens who need to be brought to a civilised state.

He is still acutely aware that his views do not accord with those of his fellow plantation owners, and keenly feels their none too subtle criticism. This seems to account for his risky visit to their club to confront his critics face to face. In chapter 6, Mr Whitechapel's inner and outer voices reflect the torment he goes through in visiting the club. The death of Chapel is cited as evidence that he does not truly enact his high-blown moral precepts and thus is, in the final analysis, but one of them. In the end, he believes that he has been absolved of his sense of guilt and hypocrisy, '*At last, I am without shame. My name is restored to me.*' (p. 78).

He is still very wary of slaves breaking out of the accepted mould, and so is uncompromising in his response when he sees Chapel reading Shakespeare to his own cherished daughter, Lydia. His orders to the two young romantics are clear and absolute, echoing the attitudes of writers to *The Virginian* who distrust the notion of black slaves being taught to read and write. However, he does not punish the young Chapel but simply verbally admonishes both he and Lydia.

In the end, we probably view him to have an 'idealised' notion of the system of slavery, where both blacks and whites have a clear sense of propriety and their place in the scheme of society. We can readily appreciate from where his most loyal slave, Whitechapel, has acquired his life philosophy, one that ultimately brings his downfall. In a sense both of them delude themselves about the real state of the system of slavery at this period in history.

Sanders Senior

Sanders Senior, who has utter contempt for the slaves he oversees, is a man whose public face is hard and unyielding. However, as we observe in his diary extracts, the private self of this brutal slaver is a far cry from his outer persona. Here is a man who is trying to come to terms with the untimely death of his young wife who presumably died in childbirth. He is man without the gentility of spirit to be able to be a proper parent, in a world where gender stereotypes are absolute. He desperately longs for a woman to be mother to his young son and a homemaker. Moreover, the arrival of the young, nubile Cook reminds him of his other unfulfilled need as a man; his long-unsatiated and insistent sexual appetite.

The voice we hear is that of a man who finds it hard to reconcile the world in which he lives with his own experience. He is fascinated by the senior slave Whitechapel, noting that 'he is by far the best worker, and he has the most agreeable manner' (p. 37). He finds himself at odds with his boss, Mr Whitechapel, over the appropriate treatment of slaves, arguing that 'cattle need fattening not slaves' (p. 38). His total lack of respect for the black slaves whom he oversees, then, places him in stark contrast to his employer.

Ironically, Sanders' views emulate those of other plantation owners. He is bewildered by Mr Whitechapel's insistence that he 'exercises restraint' (p. 41) when disciplining slaves. His young son perspicaciously asks him why he is unable to make Whitechapel's special knots if slaves are so inferior, something dismissed as no measure of ability. Sanders Junior does not naturally seem to share his father's racist views on this subject and the fact that Sanders Senior must teach his impressionable son to adopt these values and views reminds us that racism is not inherent and need not necessarily be automatically passed down from generation to generation.

The arrival of Cook into his household causes him growing consternation, both because of the natural way in which she assumes the effective role of housekeeper (though only a young girl in reality), and because of his increasingly insistent lust for her. He notes that 'This Cook is definitely a woman' (p. 41). It seems that his intentions will be thwarted by the news that Whitechapel is to marry this young, desirable and nubile girl. He is thoroughly resentful of this notion asserting: 'What does Whitechapel want with a wife. Twelve daughters is enough for one man, several men. Use one of them for comfort' (p. 42).

As Sanders Senior's resentment builds, he becomes increasingly obsessed with Cook, even dreaming of a sexual encounter with her. He acts to delay her marriage to the prolifically fathering Whitechapel. After a failed attempt to entice the innocent and virginal Cook into his bed, he finally rapes her on Christmas Eve, a suitably ironic night for a professed Christian. Cook's refusal to take any of his wife's belongings as 'payment' for her sexual favours and public silence and her instant request to marry

Whitechapel, shows us not only her love and respect for the much older Whitechapel, but also indicates the moral righteousness of this young, ill-educated black woman. She even taunts him that should he refuse to allow the marriage to occur, she would tell her Whitechapel of her assault and he would then kill Sanders Senior. He subsequently scoffs at such an idea, although at their marriage on the first day of the New Year, he acknowledges the extent of his bloodline, which permeates the slave stock on their plantation, musing, 'What if they turned against us all?' (p. 45).

A mere eight days later, Sanders Senior again rapes the vulnerable and highly accessible new bride, Cook, who valiantly tries to fend him off, even biting him. This time there are several momentous consequences: she tells her husband, who subsequently informs Mr Whitechapel; he is effectively fined by his employer; Cook becomes pregnant to him as a result of this second assault; he vows to her never to repeat the act; and he is obliged to marry again a woman he despises or lose his position as Overseer.

So, it seems Sanders Senior falls victim — in his terms at least — to the relatively benevolent attitudes that his employer has towards his slaves. No elements of brutality will be tolerated, be they to disobedient male slaves or to alluring female slaves. It is clear here that the Whitechapel Plantation is quite unlike others around it.

Sanders Junior

Significantly, in the final numbered chapter, we encounter Sanders Junior, the man who destroys both the life of his half-brother Chapel and old Whitechapel's will to live. Both he and his father have irrevocably scarred the Whitechapel clan. Ironically, it is through Sanders Junior that we learn of Whitechapel's death as he directly addresses the dead and inert body of the centenarian Whitechapel. He readily shows both his sincere regret and his genuine care for the old slave, 'I like you, though I struck you with these very hands. I'll dig your grave. I hit you because you didn't know when to hold your peace' (p. 129). He recognises that Mr Whitechapel will feel that this old man's death is a bad sign because he 'thought as long as [Whitechapel] was around the plantation would profit' (p. 132)

Sanders Junior shows his sincere respect and admiration for the old man, also acknowledging that his father felt likewise. He ends his chapter with the ultimate accolade: 'If you were white I would have wanted you as my father' (p. 134). In fact, for Sanders Junior who was denied the affection and expressed love of parents, the strength that he observes in this man makes him seem the ideal father. Old Whitechapel has shown the young Sanders Senior how to do all sorts of tricks and provided him with the attention and time that Sanders Junior so longed for from his emotionally disturbed and externally hardened father.

He marvels at the fact that Whitechapel could have raised a son with a 'wild' spirit which was so contrary to his own 'tame' one, although he acknowledges the fact that Chapel was, in reality, Sanders Senior's son, 'the son you reared' (p. 132). He realises that this old slave was a truly remarkable man, whose nobility of spirit and constancy were redoubtable in every sense. He notes that he was 'a slave unto death' (p. 132) whose life was never his in reality since his work was all 'to make Mr Whitechapel richer' (p. 132), not for his own benefit. He concludes that he would never have wanted to have lived the life that Whitechapel did — essentially because he never had a life of his own: ' A good slave, but a slave however one chooses to look at it' (p. 133).

As he gazes down upon the curled shape of this old black slave he muses upon his own brutal hand that he showed towards the man brought up as Whitechapel's son, the man who was actually his own half-brother. He notes that his own father would ironically have approved of such a 'firm hand' (p. 133) and that he thinks like his own father. Yet he cannot, it seems, admire his father or think of him with a sense of admiration. Accordingly, he wants to cover the lifeless form of old Whitechapel with his own jacket, symbolically protecting and comforting him, and reflecting the respect he had for this supposedly inferior black slave. Whilst his father may have perceived 'ambiguity towards a slave...as a sign of weakness' (p. 133), Sanders Junior is quite prepared to show his respect and admiration openly for the dead elder statesman of the plantation; the interdependency of slave and overseer seems complete in this respect.

Power of Memory

As the title *The Longest Memory* signifies, the notion of memory, its power and its resonance through time permeate much of the book. Structurally, Whitechapel's notion of memory is captured in his reflections which are contained in the 'bookends' of the 'Remembering' and 'Forgetting' sections. For Whitechapel memory is hurtful, 'like crying' (p. 2). Memory links him to a past that reminds him of his life's worst action — the betrayal of his loved son, Chapel, an act he wishes to deny and certainly forget. For Mr Whitechapel, memory can be seen as the thread in the carpet which creates the history that links and entwines people on his plantation in increasingly complex ways. For him too memory cannot be forgotten, but in his case it is because it can act as a guide to responsible behaviour. Memory enables us to recognise the importance of the past for the present.

However, above all, the central character, old Whitechapel, is by virtue of his exceptional longevity, a living testament to memory. He indeed represents links between the past, present and even perhaps the future. He was enslaved as a young ten-year-old boy in Africa and transported to the New World of America with its rigid and brutal world of the vast plantations of the Deep South. He still possesses powerful memories of these experiences. Moreover, Whitechapel, named such by the current master's father, soon came to adopt the dictum — learn through the bitter mistakes of others rather than having to repeat their often costly errors — something he tries in vain to teach his own adopted wayward son. Mr Whitechapel, his white owner, sees him as a human talisman, a living symbol of the sense of continuity between the past and the present, whose longevity reflects and somehow protects the ongoing prosperity of the Whitechapel Plantation.

This text reminds us that we never exist in isolation from the past. As time is a continuum there is always a relationship between the past and present. We find ourselves implicated in the past by our connections with it. Likewise, all of these main characters are in some sense linked by the memories of both individuals and groups within this rigidly segregated and racist society. Memory is a linking motif across the generations, as individuals either seek to justify — or to challenge — the prevailing social order. Whilst the plantation owners seek to reassert their moral justification for both slavery and their harsh treatment of their slaves, Lydia and Chapel want to overturn the existing order. Their desire is based not only upon their observations of the world as they know it, but also upon the memories they are made aware of by Whitechapel and the idealised notions of the world as contained in great works of literature.

Moreover, memory has the capacity to be both destructive and positive for individuals. Initially, Whitechapel seems to be reassured and empowered in his position on the plantation by virtue of 'memory'. At first he sees memory as an agent of pain — 'Memory hurts...Don't make me remember' (p. 2) but he concludes that 'memory is pain trying to resurrect itself' (p. 137). This view of memory is true for Whitechapel on two grounds: because of the memory of 'the pointless death' (p. 2) of Chapel, and because he has also lost many loved ones — 'two wives and most of [his] children' (p. 8). Subsequently, however, it is both his own memory and that of his fellow slaves of his complicity over the horrific death of his only son that condemns and ultimately destroys him.

Mr Whitechapel is also haunted and morally troubled by the untimely death of Chapel in his absence, and finds himself taunted by his fellow plantation owners. Sanders Senior is plagued by the memory of his dead and clearly much-loved and missed wife, Caroline, and is unable to tell his young son the truth of her death. He is subsequently confronted with his rape and assault of Cook, which becomes a nightmarish memory as he is not only forced to pay a fine but also is obligated to marry a woman he despises. Cook is haunted by her two violent rapes by Sanders Senior, the man whose house and young child she keeps so dutifully. However, she has the ameliorating and constant memory of the dutiful and unremitting love of her own beloved and noble husband, Whitechapel. Lydia relishes the ongoing memory of her mutual love for Chapel and the origins of their love. Chapel is also buoyed by the memory of his love for Lydia, yet angered too by the racism which not only surrounds him, but which is just as readily accepted by his father and by most slaves. Great Grandfather's memories of his pre-slave life in distant Africa fascinate his great granddaughter, while his role in the death of Chapel angers and puzzles her. Finally, Sanders Junior is both troubled by his own vicious treatment of his old Whitechapel and his own half-brother, as well as being reminded of his admiration for the old slave, whom he respected more than his own father.

Memory is the thread that links events for characters. Much behaviour finds it motivation in the memory of past actions and the individuals' interpretations of those events. Slavery, with its cheap labour has enabled the plantation owners to become extremely rich. They build on past methods of keeping slaves in their place to secure their wealth and so oppose change. However, slaves and others who see the injustices of the past — through direct experience, remembered or re-told — will use these memories as a basis for change to improve their lives. Memory is an active agent for present actions, thoughts and behaviours as it enables reflection on all issues, personal and public.

Racial Superiority

The belief or claim that one race is superior to another, a key theme in this text, is the basis of racism. To justify superiority, or inferiority, simply on the basis of racial origins or racial characteristics such as the colour of skin or cultural differences is now perceived to be based on prejudice. D'Aguiar clearly intends to remind us of the moral and indeed religious justification that these white, allegedly practising Christians, gave for their unspeakable racism. Whilst in the 1990s the idea that any one race could enslave another race and say that they were effectively being considerate or thoughtful seems outrageous. However, we need to remember that our modern notions of racial equality are quite recent; indeed, current waves of anti-Asian feeling in Australia should serve as a timely reminder that racism is often not far hidden, even today.

When we reflect upon the main characters in the novel, it is abundantly clear that the basis of race should not be seen to be a determinant of moral, intellectual or personality-centred superiority. Until his fateful intervention, which tragically propels his much-loved son to his brutal death, Whitechapel is much admired and respected by all those around him; he seems to be the 'elder statesman' of the slaves and is described by Mr Whitechapel and Sanders Senior as being noble and totally admirable. He clearly holds a position of respect within the hierarchy of the plantation as a whole; Sanders Junior, for example, even acknowledges that he was 'a better overseer' (p.130). Cook sees him as the best possible husband, evident in his constancy towards her, even in the face of her rape and subsequent pregnancy, and his gentle love for her. If race, for example — African, and skin colour indicate something worse than simple inferiority — something lower than humans as whites such as Sanders Senior and the plantation owners claim — then how can a Whitechapel possibly gain this respect and admiration from people as diverse as Sanders

Senior, Sanders Junior and Mr Whitechapel himself? They are unable to perceive the contradiction in their thinking.

By contrast, it seems hard to admire Sanders Senior, a man who is brutal to slaves, sees them as virtual animals, and also considers that Mr Whitechapel is far too gentle and generous in his treatment of their slaves. Here is a man who also views women as mere sex objects or housekeepers for his self-satisfaction. Likewise, if we contrast and compare the characters of Chapel and Sanders Junior, it is apparent that our sympathies and admiration are far more attuned to the former, with his sensitivity, capacity for love and morality. We reject the gruff and rather bitter slave overseer, who seems so reminiscent of his decidedly reprehensible father.

Sanders Senior by contrast reveals his brutal attitudes to slaves in many ways showing his unquestioned racism. He declares'...we are different from slaves in intelligence and human standing before God' (p. 39). Sexually, he sees no need for slaves to follow a code of moral conduct — he rapes Cook and suggests that Whitechapel should use his daughters to 'comfort him' (p. 42), that is, for sexual gratification. His inhumanity is apparent in his reference to slaves as stock at the market, highlighting that slavery is a business where humans are bought and sold, and in the punishment of 200 lashes he administers to a runaway slave who subsequently dies.

The plantation owners indicate their racist attitudes firstly in accepting and promoting slavery as an acceptable form of cheap labour. As it has become an accepted way of life only characters such as Lydia, Chapel and belatedly, Whitechapel, question it. While Mr Whitechapel sees the wisdom of making his slaves happy and prides himself on the smooth running of his plantation, he does not really think it should be abandoned as a source of cheap labour. He does acknowledge though that they are human: 'Africans may be our inferiors, but they exhibit the same qualities we possess, even if they are just imitating us'. They need to be treated 'as subjects of God, though blessed with lesser faculties, and therefore suited to the trade of slavery' (p. 32).

Above all, it is the close spiritual, intellectual and loving relationship between Lydia and Chapel that challenges any racist separation of humans for the reader. Their bond which, though undoubtedly idealistic and improbable, is surely one which appropriately parallels that which they both so admire — Shakespeare's tragic tale of pure young forbidden love in Romeo and Juliet. Indeed, on Lydia's own admission, Chapel is

far superior to any of the socially acceptable white suitors that
eagerly puts before her in an attempt to get her to do her
daughter of the master of the Whitechapel Plantation.

Slavery and Christian Values

> *It should be possible to* treat *a slave with Christian fairness and* instruct *him in the Christian faith as a just substitute for his pagan practices, without nullifying the relationship of master and slave. It has to be. Otherwise Christianity could not be spread. Otherwise the African would be deemed our equal simply because he shared our faith in one God and the Afterlife. We both know of the above to be false because of the evidence of how Africans live in their primitive land. (p. 111)*

The views expressed in this quotation suggest how slave-owners and traders attempted to justify and rationalise their treatment of their black slaves as being good or Christian. By labelling their fellow humans who are of a different race and skin colour as 'uncivilised' and 'inferior', they could then justly (in their terms) treat them as the equivalent of animal stock, presumably training them to be 'better' creatures. Given the Christian emphasis upon equality and brotherly love these attitudes seem especially hard to fathom. Unfortunately, past and present events remind us that any religion or set of moral beliefs can be adjusted or shifted to accommodate practical or pragmatic considerations all too easily.

Chapter 6, with its confrontation between Mr Whitechapel and his fellow plantation owners, presents a clear insight into the inherent conflict these elements present. Mr Whitechapel has relatively humanitarian views with respect to his treatment of his slaves, most pointedly shown in his reaction to the rape of Cook and his upholding of a moral position even when it involves a young black female slave. He has real admiration for his namesake old slave, and, it seems, is always prepared to listen to his counsel and advice. He shuns the overtly brutal actions of both his colleagues and slave overseers, and sees no real conflict of interest between his avowed Christianity and his use and dependence upon the labour of slaves. In fact, the plantation owners argue that slavery is a business concerned with their 'physical and material well-being; while Christianity looks after the hunger of the soul' (p.111). The arguments, however, are admitted to be on shaky grounds for the editor admits 'that once we

…nd Christian values to include slaves we then throw into question …e very basis of our forced enslavement of them' (p. 111). Nevertheless, he and the plantation owners continue to assert their power over slaves demonstrating that self-interest blinds them to arguments of justice and equality inherent in Christian beliefs.

Mr Whitechapel's views lie between those of the plantation owners and his own daughter's for he cannot accept Lydia's truly Christian libertarian views. She believes that slaves ought to be emancipated and then hired and paid for their labour as properly acknowledged workers and that inter-racial 'liaisons' are absolutely acceptable. Her views of course especially challenge the prevailing 'orthodoxy', which perceives black slaves to be incapable of love with whites since they are lesser creatures with less civilising qualities.

In the end, we can only condemn these espoused Christians who so blatantly enslave other humans and treat them so appallingly, whilst supposedly believing Christianity's fundamental tenets.

There have been many other examples of theoretically religious people advocating practices that we now find to be utterly repugnant. For approximately 90 years, the policy of 'Apartheid' (separate development according to race) ensured that many black South Africans were effectively little better than black slaves in their own country, with almost no legal rights or protection from often horrific exploitation by unscrupulous whites.

Riches through Others' Misery

D'Aguiar points to that most obvious, and yet oft overlooked of moral dilemmas: the notion that one group of people can be permitted to grow rich through the misery and hard manual labour of others. Without the physically hard work and sheer size of its black slave workforce, the Deep South would never have produced the affluent plantation region it did. Naturally, this accounts for the vehemence with which the Southerners rejected the anti-slave movements of the Northern Unionist states and which lay at the heart of the entire Civil War. The predominant images from these plantations were of masses of slaves toiling from daybreak to dusk, with few breaks, sometimes even in chains and singing plaintive 'spirituals' of their misery and fundamental sadness.

Whilst Mr Whitechapel undoubtedly wants to portray his plantation to be a gentler and more humane place than most of its neighbouring ones, the inescapable fact remains that he and his family and overseers get rich through the enforced labour of their slave workforce. Moreover, their comfortable lifestyle is ensured by the use of black house-servants. Had they the option, would these black slaves seriously entertain the idea of working so hard to ensure that their white bosses could live such an affluent lifestyle whilst they themselves endured a host of deprivations and hardships? Both the other plantation owners and Sanders Senior muse upon the frightening spectre of their abundant black workforce rising up against them in mutiny.

Powerlessness of Women

Women in earlier centuries endured a host of forms of inequality and injustice. This novel highlights the dominance of males in many facets of life in the Deep South, especially through the characters of Lydia and Cook, but also indirectly through Caroline Sanders and Mrs Whitechapel. Lydia represents a new-age woman, one who refuses to accept silently the pre-determined positions of her social status and family. She is not prepared to play automatically the role of the 'Southern Belle', with a simpering manner, inane small talk, a belief in men to be the superior gender and a willingness to shuffle across a room in a helpless and genteel manner. Moreover, Lydia perceives it to be her own right to determine who her husband ought to be, and to marry for love rather than dynastic or practical convenience. Whilst her mother may want her to use the great works of literature which grace their library as means to achieve graceful steps across a room, Lydia desires them as means of inner intellectual nourishment. Lydia seems to want the independence of self-determination women today automatically expect, which is rather patronisingly noted by the editor of *The Virginian*.

Cook, on the other hand, is a female victim in another crucial way, namely sexually. Her totally unprovoked assault and two experiences of rape by her white master, represents the ultimate form of brutal assault by any man over a woman. Cook is a young, virginal and clearly alluring young black woman who quickly gains the attention of both Sanders Senior and the aged Whitechapel. The latter still longs for female companionship and the elusive son after thirteen daughters. She is utterly defenceless against the advances of either man, though, of course, the moral and decent Whitechapel, we readily understand, would never 'take advantage' of a woman. Moreover, the age-old 'double standard' applies here potentially; the view that any woman who has been in a sexual encounter must have 'led the man on' and is therefore culpable, certainly not to be pitied. Were it not for Whitechapel's generosity of spirit, Cook would have been cast adrift by others in her pregnant state, despite her total innocence. Such is the lot of women in the 18th century.

Likewise, Caroline Sanders, the dead first wife of Sanders Senior and mother to his only son, is a victim in another way. Her untimely death has been presumably caused by the prevalent risks of childbirth; risks which were all too common until after the Second World War in this century. Moreover, reflecting upon the attitudes of her mourning husband, it is clear that she has had little life of her own when alive.

Further, Mrs Whitechapel, as a dutiful wife, fulfils the roles her husband expects of her as the mistress of the plantation. As a consequence she is obliged to subjugate any desires she may have for intellectual pursuits, career or independence. She is expected to be totally dependent upon her husband in almost every sense, other than raising their children when young and managing the day-to-day running of the plantation house.

Power of Literacy

As long ago as feudal times, rulers and those in power became acutely aware of the immense power given to individuals through literacy (the ability to read and write) for with it comes the liberating power of being able to influence others and to advocate political change. To intentionally keep the 'peasants' ignorant and hungry is a long-honoured tradition of control. Even in relatively recent times this practice has been seen under the former racist policy of apartheid ('separate development') in South Africa, where black Africans were not even able to learn the same language as that of the ruling whites (Afrikaans). So it is that the white slave owners of this novel deliberately refuse to allow their black slaves to become literate, ostensibly because they are incapable of such intellectual learning. The real reason, however, has far more to do with control and power. This is most apparently seen in Mr Whitechapel's outrage and horror at encountering his own beloved daughter Lydia, 'the darling of the house', hearing young Chapel read to her in a swoon. For him, this represents the ultimate transgression of the gulf between the two races; reflected in the comments of the editor of *The Virginian* (p. 117) about blacks' ability to read and write.

Chapel is the key character upon whom to focus in this context since he is not only highly literate thanks to the personal tuition of Lydia, but also because he is able to use language in one of its highest and most sophisticated forms, poetry. Further, as he is of mixed racial background, he has an affinity with both sides of the divide. Chapel, through his verse, is able to encapsulate much of the inherent tension and discontent which underscores Southern society as slavery begins to come under challenge. He shows enormous insights, and his inner voice reflects the psychological hurt and spiritual disharmony of the lifestyle of slaves.

The Power of Love

A perennial theme, which runs through this novel, is that of the strength and impetus generated by loving relationships. Despite the horror of slavery in the Deep South, there are many forms of love observable to the reader, which act as a positive and empowering element in people's lives.

The idyllic love of Lydia and Chapel has a pure and virtuous quality reminiscent of Shakespeare's 'star-crossed lovers', Romeo and Juliet. It helps them to rise above the nature of their situation and to dream of an ideal world in which race and skin colour no longer dictate the terms of people's lives. It represents a socially inappropriate liaison to both sets of parents, as it runs contrary to the entire fabric of the world in which they live. The newspaper editor to whom Lydia writes is especially condemnatory of such inter-racial relationships, asserting that, 'there is no sight more perfidious than that of a white woman with a black man' (p.120). The love of these two young people helps them to cope with the system in which they find themselves and which they both find so repugnant.

The love of the aged Whitechapel for the young Cook is a redeeming and life-giving force to both of them. Without it, Cook would never have been able to cope with her horrific assaults by Sanders Senior. As she herself concludes, 'Whitechapel is my life...There is no earthly way I can match his love' (p. 55). Likewise, the aged Whitechapel seems rejuvenated by his young bride and reactivated by his obvious love for her. Even Sanders Senior in his diaries reveals a deep love for his first wife, Caroline and his emotionally and sexually bereft state after her death.

Love's transforming power is therefore central to key relationships in this novel. Significantly, it is only in inter-racial and black relationships that we are presented with such positive and invigorating loving relationships.

Sample Exam Questions

1. 'Lydia is really attracted to Chapel since he represents what her white suitors can never hope to become — a hopeful visionary.' Do you agree?
2. 'Both Whitechapel and Mr Whitechapel delude themselves about the world that really surrounds them.' Discuss.
3. 'The belief in the need to keep a disadvantaged group illiterate and ignorant is a time-honoured and powerful mechanism of unjust control.' Discuss fully in the context of *The Longest Memory*.
4. 'Whitechapel may be stabilising force on this Virginian plantation, but his influence, like his life, cannot last forever.' Do you agree?
5. 'The power of memory can be a negative as well as a positive force.' Does your reading of the novel support this view?
6. 'Lydia's determination not to pursue the life which has been set down for her reflects both her need for independence as well as for true love.' Do you agree?
7. 'The fabric that has been woven between Whitechapel, Mr Whitechapel, Sanders, Chapel and Cook is so entwined that any individual disaster is bound to enmesh them all'. Explore in relation to Chapel.
8. How does the way the story is told add to our understanding of the text? (VCE English Exam Paper, 1997, p. 11)
9. 'The master is daylight, the slave is night. A complete day needs both light and dark.' How does the writer highlight the interdependence of slave and master…? (VCE English Exam Paper, 1997, p.11)

Analysing a Sample Question

NOTE: This is NOT a model answer!

Read the sample answer then discuss the questions below.

Topic: 'The power of memory can be negative as well as a positive force.'

Answer: The power of memory is immense. Not only does our memory provide us with an opportunity to define our past but it also is a powerful tool that indirectly shapes our futures. As Whitechapel muses, 'The future is just more of the past waiting to happen'.

In the novel, *The Longest Memory*, characters use memory in different ways, and, in turn, memory influences and affects them differently. This reinforces the notion that the power of memory can be both a negative as well as a positive force.

Take, for instance, Whitechapel — master slave and oldest man on the Whitechapel plantation. For Whitechapel, his own memory becomes a burden to retain. Whitechapel feels bound to repress his painful past and refuses to consciously remember on account of the possibility of more of the past recurring. Indeed, Whitechapel has had a tragic past, filled with turmoil. He has lost his young second wife due to illness, as well as Chapel, the longed-for boy he took as his own son. For this he holds himself accountable. His son's death upsets the whole world which otherwise appears unshakeable. Whitechapel says that he has, 'learned to live without being hurt by life' and that he has 'seen enough for one life, several enough in fact.'

Whitechapel's memory increasingly causes him anguish and drives him to despair. He wears an awful sense of culpability and responsibility for what he has unintentionally brought to bear upon his only son, Chapel. To nullify this anguish, Whitechapel severs his links with his memories to cope with this horrible problem, thereby removing his sensitivity and creating a barrier that protects him from the pain created through remembering.

These memories even affect Whitechapel's physical state. Mentally we know he is under immense strain, however the effects of this also bring about a physical deterioration. 'There are lines, two of them, on each side of Whitechapel's mouth...that run from the corner of his lips, down his chin, as deep as a scar.' Everyone comes to call him 'Sour-face'. Worry has etched those lines into his face out of these painful memories. Also, the way Whitechapel acts, and the other slaves' memory of Chapel's death, cause them to now treat Whitechapel with disrespect, claiming that he 'betrayed' Chapel. They almost treat him with contempt, as a waste of space. These situations, created by memory, have certainly acted as a negative force on Whitechapel, thus verifying the hypothesis in this statement.

Whitechapel is not the only person within the novel for whom memory exerts a powerful impact. Whitechapel's son, Chapel, in contrast to Whitechapel, relies upon memory for intellectual fulfilment and stimulation, as well as for pleasure. Chapel uses Lydia's memory as a vehicle for a freedom of sorts. She memorises passages from the books and poetry they both so admire. Chapel wants to remember as much as possible, since as well as providing him with enjoyment and knowledge, he wants to show that he is worthy of these great literary classics. He uses the memory of this literature to lessen the burden of his tragic memories, that is, his mother's illness and Lydia and his dilemma.

Ironically, the freedom created by Chapel's literacy is a forbidden asset for slaves to acquire. Chapel generally uses his memory in a positive way, further adding weight to the notion that memory can be a positive force.

Paradoxically, Mr Whitechapel's memory acts as both a positive and a negative force. His memory becomes a moral judge. When he travels to the plantation owners'club, he is dogged by his conscience, feeling that he must 'weather the shame'. However, he then recalls the memory of his father and the positive manner in which they have both fought for their values and run the plantation according to their principles, regardless of the discontent of their peers. In this way, Mr Whitechapel's memory gives him the strength to fight to clear his name with these vocal critics. Reacting to his conscience in this way strengthens his character. It is his thoughtfulness and due consideration of those around him that makes Mr Whitechapel the respected, moral plantation owner that he is; the clear distinguishing characteristic from the other stereotypical plantation owners.

Therefore, it is clear that the power of memory can be a negative as well as a positive force in people's lives. As readers, we are able to see the truth in this hypothesis. [Approximately 730 words]

Discussion questions

- Does the opening here appropriately focus on the given topic?
- Is there an apparent thorough understanding of the topic throughout?
- Does the essay develop logically and sequentially?
- Is appropriate and adequate detail from the text provided?
- Is there a sense of personal engagement with the text that engages the reader?

VITAL EXAM STRATEGIES

In the final end-of-year exam, you will have to write a response on two different texts from the official Board of Studies text list for study. Each of the 30 set texts will have two individual analytical topics provided on the exam paper. Such an analytical essay requires you to:

- Demonstrate your close and precise working knowledge of the text in question, including several brief and succinct quotations, or references to specific elements of the text, as are appropriate to the chosen topic
- Present and develop a clear and relevant line of argument in response to the topic
- Resolve the chosen topic, in line with your own reading of the text
- Reveal your own personal understanding and appreciation of the text.

You must not simply list key parts of the text or merely translate or explore key aspects of the chosen topic. This is fundamentally an argumentative writing task, which also expects you to reveal your own close and thorough analysis of the text in the light of this topic.

You ought to avoid needless explanation or retelling of the actual plot. It is presumed that you have fully understood the text and its component parts — as has your audience for this essay. The only details about the text, which ought to be given here, are those that support and reinforce the argument you have developed in response to your selected topic.

The three key areas of assessment criteria are the:

- Depth of textual knowledge
- Quality and appropriateness of structure
- Quality and control of all aspects of expression.

Above all else, your answer must be directly relevant to the whole topic.

See Ross Huggard's CAT 3: Your Guide to the English Exam 1998 *(Insight Publications) for answers to your questions about the exam, more on exam study strategies, and assessor comments on student answers.*

REFERENCES & READING

Text

D'Aguiar, Fred, *The Longest Memory*, Vintage, Random House, Sydney, 1995

References on the Novel

Allen, John, *The Longest Memory, Notes for Teachers*, Random House, Australia, 1996

Contemporary Authors, Gale Research, Michigan, 1996, Vol. 148

Lonsdale, Michele, Review in *The Age*, 'Student Update' 13/5/97

Metcalf, Mary-Ann, *Fred D'Aguiar Author Interview*, Random House, Australia, 1996

Further Readings

Attwood, Alan, 'Gone with the flames', *The Age*, 22/6/96

Clough, Juliet, 'In Scarlett's Footsteps', *The Age*, Travel section, 5/4/97

Gilbey, Emma, 'Children: new recruits of the Ku Klux Klan', in *Time*, Report USA, April 1996

Mansfield, Paul, 'Slaves to laughter', *The Age*, Travel section, 4/10/97

Internet

Harrison, Katharine, Review in *The New Reader,* Vol.XV, Number 2, Summer 1995 <http://www.literascape.com>.